Bob Artley's

Country
Christmas

As Remembered by a Former Kid

Voyageur Press

To my family

Bob Artley has retired on the farm near Hampton, Iowa, that was his boyhood home. That farm, in the Artley family for more than a century, appears in this book.

Bob began drawing as a boy, encouraged by the *Des Moines Register and Tribune*'s great cartoonist Ding Darling. He studied art formally at Grinnell College and the University of Iowa. His career as an editorial cartoonist began at the *Des Moines Tribune* and continued at the *Worthington* (Minnesota) *Daily Globe*. Bob has also worked in advertising and, with his wife Ginny, published two weekly papers.

Theoretically retired, Bob continues to write, draw, and paint. His most recent books are a memoir, *Ginny: A Love Remembered*, and an affectionate look at bygone farm objects, *Country Things*.

First published in 2006 by Voyageur Press, an imprint of MBI Publishing Company, Galtier Plaza, Suite 200, 380 Jackson Street, St. Paul, MN 55101-3885 USA

MBI Publishing Company titles are also available at discounts in bulk quantity for industrial or sales-promotional use. For details write to Special Sales Manager at MBI Publishing Company, Galtier Plaza, Suite 200, 380 Jackson Street, St. Paul,
MN 55101-3885 USA

Artley, Bob.
  [Country Christmas]
  Bob Artley's Country Christmas : as remembered by a former kid / by Bob Artley.
      p. cm.
  Originally published: Country Christmas, as remembered by a former kid. Ames : Iowa State University Press, 1994.
  ISBN-13: 978-0-7603-2652-7 (plc w/ jacket)
  ISBN-10: 0-7603-2652-5 (plc w/ jacket)
  1. Christmas—Iowa. 2. Iowa—Social life and customs. 3. Artley, Bob—Anecdotes. I. Title.
  GT4986.I8A77 2006
  394.266309777--dc22
Printed in China

Contents

Preface

Christmas comes but once a year,
And when it comes it brings good cheer.

This little playground ditty became a part of my Christmas lore during my country school years. However, the beauty, magic, and wonder of that special season had been well established in my store of memories long before starting school.

In the ambience of our loving farm home, it was easy for my brothers and me to understand the central theme of Christmas. The manger scene was one that we could easily relate to, familiar as we were with barns. We even knew about birth in a stable (of our farm animals) and felt that all of the creatures on the farm should share in some way our joy.

Even as children, I believe we had an understanding of the humble origins of the Christmas story. Not only could we relate to the stable scene, but we too knew what it was to have limited means. Not that we felt poor (even though by today's standards we would have been considered below the poverty level), but we knew that the exciting toys, so tantalizingly depicted in the pages of the mail-order catalogs, were fun to look at and dream over but were not actually ours to possess.

We knew from experience that there would be some Christmas surprises for us under the decorated tree. However, the Christmas spirit was not solely dependent upon the presents we received but included the total atmosphere expressed in carols, cards, music, decorations, fragrances, feasts, and family gatherings. Christmas was a time of loving companionship—goodwill toward all.

Artley Farm
Hampton, Iowa

Country Christmas

A Long Ago
Christmas on the Farm

ARTLEY '80

Christmas memories of childhood on the farm are particularly rich, in spite of the fact that they are of a time that was short of cash with little of the material comforts we think are so necessary for happiness today.

For weeks before the celebration of the great event, we spent hours going through the pages of the mail-order catalogs "ah-ing" and "oh-ing" over the illustrations of things we would like to have. We didn't expect to get all— or maybe any—of the things pictured and described, but it was fun looking. We knew, however, that there would be something for each of us under the tree Christmas morning, given in love and received in appreciation.

But more important than the gifts was the magic of the season. Its spirit pervaded everything we did as we prepared for the great day. Our chores, homework, and even school itself were favorably affected by the atmosphere of that wonderful season.

Besides poring over the pages of the catalog, we got out the box of Christmas decorations, made some new decorations, and helped get the house ready for Christmas. We played "Silent Night" over and over again on our scratchy old Victrola. We also made our own music as we went about the chores singing and whistling our repertoire of carols. We learned our parts for the Christmas programs. And, if we had the necessary coins, we bought presents for our parents and grandparents and one another. Many times we had to make them small gifts.

Christmas, during those long ago years, included celebrations at school, church, Grandma Artley's in town, and at Grandpa and Grandma Crow's on their farm. These were all great fun, especially when it meant traveling by bobsled. However, of those blessed Christmases when we were small, it is the memories of those times spent at home on the farm that retain the most meaning down through the years.

As we drove down the lane in the bobsled to spend Christmas Eve at Grandma's house and at church, I glanced back at the familiar cluster of farm buildings. I knew that beneath the snow-covered roofs the animals were snug in the straw, warm in their winter coats. Tracks in the snow, fresh that day, traced where we had gone from building to building doing our chores. Within that dark, silent house I knew that the fire in the living room stove had been carefully banked so there would be some warmth upon our return later that night. Beneath the fragrant boughs of a simply decorated tree I knew there lay wrapped gifts to be opened in the morning. The world in which we lived was full of warmth, love, and excitement.

As Christmas Day drew near, we were forbidden to enter the workshop. After supper or at odd moments during the day, Dad, with Mom's help and encouragement, would be at his workbench making something special to put beneath the tree on Christmas morning. These special gifts over the years included a toy house and barn with cutout animals, a windmill, a set of wooden freight train cars, and a little red table with two chairs, which are still used by little visitors to the farm. Those homemade gifts, with their accompanying smell of fresh paint mingled with the fragrance of the evergreen tree, are highlights in our memories of those Christmases of long ago.

Preparations for the Christmas festivities involved the efforts of the whole family. The spirit of the season sparked our enthusiasm for doing jobs that at any other time we would have found worthy only of protesting groans. But now carrying water to the reservoir on the back of the kitchen range and keeping the firewood supply adequate in the house were part of the anticipation of the fun times ahead.

The mailbox at the end of our lane was our contact with the world beyond the farm. Through it came our daily newspaper, communication with friends and family in faraway places, magazines, and mail-order catalogs. Probably the most exciting mail was the packages that arrived during the holiday season. These mysterious parcels might be gifts from Uncle John in California or something ordered from Sears, Roebuck.

The goodwill we felt at this season included the beasts of our farm. So on the afternoon before Christmas when Dad announced we were hauling straw from the stack across the road, we were eager to help. We took special care to see that the bedding in the stalls, pens, and shed was extra deep so that the animals would have a cozy Christmas. This seemed significant to us since Christmas began in similar surroundings.

We wanted the creatures of our farm to share in our joy at Christmas. In addition to the comfort of clean stalls bedded with deep, fresh straw, we made sure that each received an extra portion of their favorite food—corn. We took special pleasure in going from pen to pen and stall to stall with their "Christmas treats."

Doing chores in winter was not pleasant. We were contending with bitter cold and snow. But there was a feeling of contentment and satisfaction in seeing to the needs and comfort of the creatures in our care. At Christmastime this feeling was more intense, as we went from the snowy farmyard on a cold December evening into the comparative warmth of the lantern-lit barn with the unique fragrance and coziness of feeding time.

Much of the preparation for Christmas fell to Mom. She supervised the decorations that went up soon after Thanksgiving Day, did most of the shopping for presents—little as that was—and of course prepared the food and extra goodies that made Christmas a time of feasting at our house. All sorts of good things were produced in Mom's kitchen throughout the year. But for the holiday season she outdid herself in making pies, cakes, cookies, popcorn balls, and two or three kinds of homemade candy in addition to the bread and special buns.

Suppertime was in many ways my favorite time of day. In winter it was an especially cozy time—the chores were done, and the family came together and shared their experiences of the day around the lamp-lit table of nourishing food and common concern. At Christmas, suppertime, like everything else, was enhanced by the spirit of the season. And Mom's kitchen, simple and without many of the conveniences even of that day, was a warm, fragrant, and wonderful place.

The tree was set up in our living room only a few days before Christmas Day. Usually it came from the spruce trees in our house yard, often fabricated from tied-together branches of those evergreens. Its fragrance made up for whatever it lacked in fullness and symmetry. Most of the decorations were made at home (tinfoil-covered cardboard stars, strings of popcorn and cranberries, or paper chains), with a small collection of items bought at the store—glass balls and bits of tinsel that were carefully unpacked and hung on the tree year after year.

This scene represents a Christmas when our brand-new baby brother lay in a crib in the adjoining bedroom, thus making the Christmas story more real to us.

A Family
Christmas

The iron runners slid and bumped over the snow-packed roads, rumbled over wooden bridges, and screeched, cold steel on cold steel, over the railroad crossings. The horses pulled the bobsled with ease, and I was glad. I liked riding, and I didn't want to think of the horses having a hard time of it for my fun. Dolly and Daisy had pulled us along in the sled for about 12 miles. I did wonder about the horses' feet. Were they as cold as mine?

We all—Mom, Dad, my brother, and I—had been made snug for the journey when we left home early that afternoon. However, by now the cold had begun to seep through our heavy wraps. Frost was forming on the scarf that covered the lower part of my face. My fingers, in the double layered mittens, were tingling with the cold. But worst of all, my toes felt like small frozen potatoes in the front end of my booted shoes. I was sure they would

spill out of my socks when I undressed them.

Suddenly the discomforts of the lengthy, open-air ride were forgotten. Over a rise in the snowy landscape appeared the familiar, long, tree-lined lane that led to Grandma and Grandpa's farmstead. We were going there for Christmas!

By the time our bobsled pulled up in front of the houseyard gate, Grandpa was on the porch pulling on his coat, and cousins appeared at the windows. The next few moments were pandemonium. We boys were out of the bobsled and up the freshly shoveled walk to be hugged by Grandpa and Grandma, then into the fragrant warmth of Grandma's kitchen to be greeted by the rest.

Grandpa helped Dad put Dolly and Daisy into the stall in the barn and gave them a generous portion of oats and timothy hay—their Christmas dinner.

And what a dinner was being prepared for *us* in Grandma's kitchen!

After our wraps had been put away and the kisses had been wiped from our cheeks (Mom's family was generous in its show of affection), we cousins went whooping through the house, anxious to view the gaily decorated Christmas tree in the parlor. A huge pile of brightly wrapped packages lay beneath its fragrant branches.

Then we flew back through the living room (where we were asked to slow down by Uncle George), around the stretched-out table with its festive setting in the dining room, and on into the kitchen to the source of those wonderful aromas.

Grandma was supervising everything. Mom and my aunts were helping with the last-minute details. There were pumpkin pies and a big bowl of whipped cream. (A surreptitious sample on the tip of the finger revealed it to be flavored with just the right amount of vanilla.) There were pickles (sliced cucumber, beet, and spiced crab apple), freshly baked buns, mashed potatoes, creamed carrots, and a large casserole of scalloped corn. Central to the whole feast was the huge turkey, beautifully browned. Grandma had just pulled it from the oven. The dressing was scooped into a serving dish and the gravy prepared.

Word was passed around that everyone should come to the table. We needed no coaxing, and the whole family was soon seated on dining chairs, kitchen chairs, the piano bench, and a kitchen stool around that groaning oak table. My brother Dean, the youngest and smallest, had to sit on the huge family Bible placed on his chair to bring him up to table height. Grandpa remarked that Dean wouldn't go wrong if he always used it as his foundation.

Then we all bowed our heads for Grandpa's

prayer of thanksgiving. Indeed, there was much to be thankful for.

When our hunger was appeased, our thoughts turned to the Christmas tree set in front of the west window in the parlor. It was somewhat spindly, but its fragrance made up for its appearance. The base of this green spruce was set in a bucket of wet sand, and this in turn was covered by a white sheet.

An impressive assortment of gaily colored tissue-wrapped packages was piled high under the branches of the tree. A little tag was attached to each package, designating for whom it was intended and from whom it came. Up in the branches nestled smaller packages and other decorations—colored glass balls, bits of tinsel, and colored paper cones filled with popcorn, peanuts, and hard candies. At the very top of the tree was a cardboard star covered with lead foil.

By the time dinner was over, the gray sky outside had turned to black and the kerosene lamps needed to be lit. While the table was cleared, leftovers put into the pantry, the dishes washed, and the milking done, we kids tried to contain our excitement in anticipation of the gift exchange. The time dragged on, and we were told repeatedly to quiet down. Aunt Ethel tried, without success, to steer us into quiet sitting games.

Finally the last dish was put away, the milk from the barn was strained and put into crocks to cool in the pantry, and everyone began to gather in the parlor. It was decided that Cousin Verl would read the tags on the packages and we smaller ones would deliver them to the persons intended.

It was a noisy, exiting time. Grandma and Grandpa were more or less accorded a place of honor, and everyone took note of the gifts they received. It

was like a multi-ring circus as everyone opened and exclaimed over their gifts.

The gifts were simple, practical things for the most part, but they seemed luxurious to us. There were brightly colored mittens of intricate design that Grandma had spent many hours knitting for the whole family. Those for the younger ones were tied together with a yarn string to keep them from becoming separated and lost. Grandpa had made spinning tops from wooden spools for thread. There were also purchased gifts—toys, slippers, scarves, shawls, delicate dishes, vases, and books—it seemed there were books for everyone.

After the last gift had been unwrapped and the last tissue wrapping paper had been either folded carefully (for next year) or stuffed into a cardboard box, Aunt Bertha started playing Christmas carols on the piano. Gradually we all gathered around, making a joyous sound in celebration of the wonderful season.

After the songfest, when things had almost calmed down, Aunt Ethel suggested how nice it would be to have a sleigh ride. The suggestion was met with enthusiasm by everyone but our family. (We had just gotten warm after our long bobsled ride that very afternoon.) Aunt Ethel, Uncle Will, and Cousin Verl were from the city, so to them it would be a treat. After some persuading by the others, we finally caught the spirit. Dad agreed to reharness Daisy and Dolly and hitch them to the bobsled.

All of us, with the exception of Grandma and Mom, bundled up in our winter wraps and piled onto the bobsled. Someone held a lighted kerosene lantern

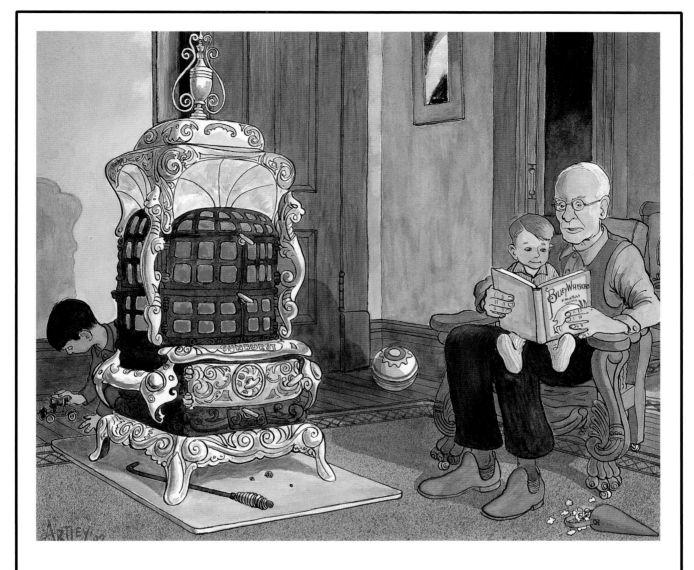

in the front and another held one in the rear. Behind the bobsled, attached by a rope, was a coaster sled on which we smaller cousins took turns riding.

Dad guided the horses in an easy trot across the farmyard and down the long lane. On either side of the lane stood large maple trees whose branches met overhead, making a "covered bridge" in the summertime.

But tonight, the trees' bare branches reached into the cold darkness of the winter night, and the lane was choked with drifts of snow. The drifts weren't large, but they caused an undulating ride in the sled. They also caused the little sled behind to dump its squealing cargo now and then. When this happened the team was stopped, the little sled was set upright and remounted, and we were off again amid much laughing and shouting.

At the end of the lane, we turned north onto the road past the farm. Our merry band formed a cozy cocoon of sound and light as we moved through the vast expanse of silence and darkness in the cold winter landscape. Now and then, a twinkling light could be seen here and there across the fields and through the groves—silent testimony to life besides ours in this snowy farmland, perhaps also celebrating Christmas.

We drove past the crossroads for about a half mile, then turned into the open gate to a field, circled back onto the road, and headed south toward home. Before long we were back in the farmyard.

Our jolly band came laughing, puffing, and stomping into the kitchen where Grandma and Mom had prepared a lunch of hot cocoa and leftovers from dinner. During the rest of the evening, the grownups visited, read from their Christmas books, or dozed in

their chairs near the warmth of the hard-coal burner. We kids tried out our toys again, and Grandpa read to us from some of our new books.

The old Seth Thomas clock on the shelf in the kitchen "bonged" nine o'clock and bedtime was decreed. We didn't mind, however, for we liked the upstairs in this old house. We climbed the stairway where we had spent hours bouncing rubber balls. The four bedrooms opening off the hallway were excellent for playing "bear," a scary version of hide and seek. In the small northeast bedroom a door led to the attic, which contained all sorts of interesting things.

We were to sleep in the southeast room in a big black walnut bed—large and sturdy enough to accommodate three lively boys who had to be reminded repeatedly to get to sleep.

Eventually, after the kerosene lamp was placed in the hall beyond our open door, things did quiet down and I became aware of the measured breathing of Dean and Harold.

As I became drowsier and drowsier, I heard the groaning of the windmill outside and the comforting sound of muffled voices from downstairs. Finally, the Seth Thomas down in the kitchen began to strike the hour of ten.

I didn't hear it finish.

Just as our one-room country school stood out on the lonely landscape, so did the Christmas season stand out in a rather monotonous school year.

School started each day at nine o'clock, and we had to run like crazy to get there before the bell stopped ringing.

Opening exercises usually conasisted of the Pledge of Allegiance and the Lord's Prayer. Sometimes Teacher read a chapter or two aloud from *The Wizard of Oz*, *Black Beauty*, or another of our favorite books.

After opening exercises, school started in earnest, some students reciting and the rest of us studying our lessons for our turn at recitation.

Along about midmorning, just when it seemed we couldn't sit still another minute, we had recess. We got all bundled up in our coats, caps, scarves, boots, and mittens and had the time of our lives playing in the snow.

BOB ARTLEY

But just when we got well into our play, the bell would ring and we would have to go back inside, get out of our coats, caps, scarves, boots, and mittens and take to learning again until noon. Then we would eat our packed lunches and get in some more play before the bell rang again.

For the older ones, the long periods of study and recitation were occasionally broken up by permission to go for coal or water.

After lunchtime there was more study and recitation, then afternoon recess, then learning again until it was time to go home, when we went "a hootin' an' hollerin'" out the door and down the road toward home.

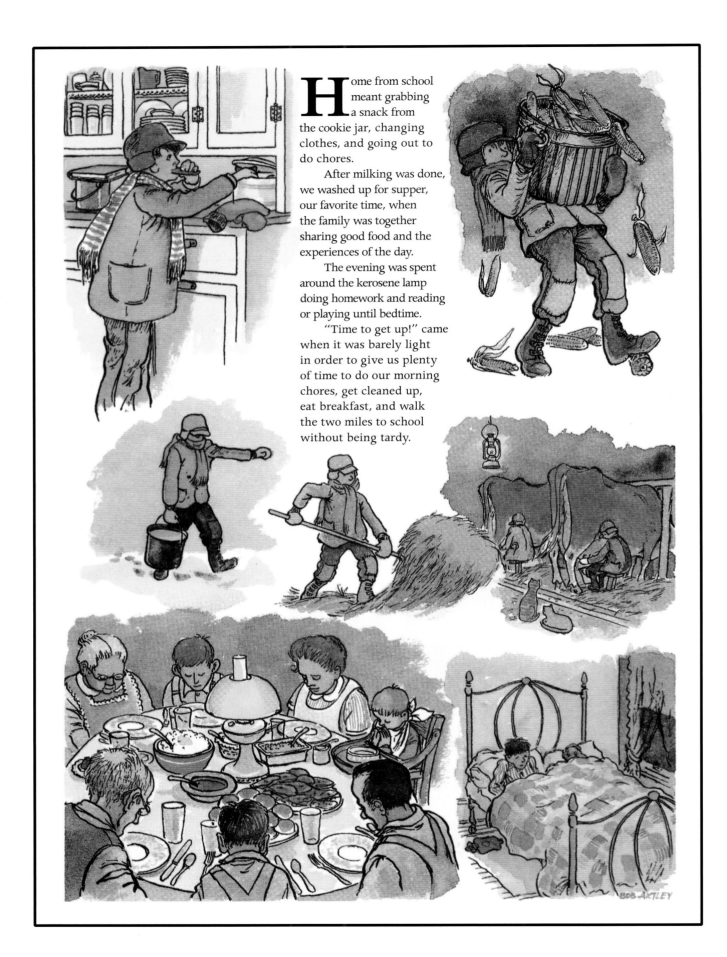

Home from school meant grabbing a snack from the cookie jar, changing clothes, and going out to do chores.

After milking was done, we washed up for supper, our favorite time, when the family was together sharing good food and the experiences of the day.

The evening was spent around the kerosene lamp doing homework and reading or playing until bedtime.

"Time to get up!" came when it was barely light in order to give us plenty of time to do our morning chores, get cleaned up, eat breakfast, and walk the two miles to school without being tardy.

This was pretty much our routine most of the school year. But as the Christmas season approached our existence changed.

Two or three weeks before Christmas our study time was cut short each day so we could prepare for that great season. We decorated our schoolroom, practiced our parts for the Christmas program, made gifts for our parents, and drew names of those for whom we would bring gifts.

A day or two before the Christmas program, the box containing the gingham curtains was brought down from the attic in the belfry. After the supporting wire was put up and the curtains strung on it, partitioning off the stage area, the atmosphere of the whole room was changed, giving a greater realism (and urgency) to our rehearsals.

BOB ARTLEY '85

E ven though Christmas Day was a week away, its magic transformed our little schoolhouse into a wondrous place. The night of the program lights from the kerosene wall lamps and borrowed gas lanterns beckoned to us through the windows as we approached in the bobsled loaded with our family, baskets of food, and presents.

It was strange to see the schoolyard crowded with cars and horses hitched to bobsleds. The schoolroom itself bore little resemblance to the one we knew so well. It was jammed with people—our parents, siblings, relatives, friends, and neighbors. They were crowded into seats too small for them, on folding chairs in the aisles and along the walls.

It seemed the program was over very soon, for all the time and effort that was put into practicing and preparation.

Some of us forgot our lines, of course, but our audience didn't seem to mind. In fact, judging by their laughter, they liked those parts best. For the finale, the teacher had everyone join in singing "Joy to the World." This seemed to help put everyone in a joyful mood for the gift exchange and lunch that followed.

The exchange of gifts that followed was only for those of us in school, but the little ones in the audience each were given something too.

One thing these gatherings always did was bring out the very best from the kitchens of the neighborhood. Four or five different kinds of sandwiches, pies, cakes, cookies, and homemade candies came from the baskets and boxes that had been stacked in the corners until this point.

Finally, the food baskets, utensils, and presents were gathered up, children were wrapped and buttoned against the cold ride home, good-byes and merry Christmases were said, cars were cranked up, and horses were roused from their standing naps. Then we all headed for our homes, leaving the little schoolhouse to stand by itself on the dark, lonely prairie.

BOB ARTLEY '85

Christmas Shopping in a Country Store

It was always fun to go into Latimer with Dad. My brother and I went at every opportunity. During the summer months our chance was likely to be on "cream days," when we took the dripping cans of cream from the cooling tanks in the milk house and hauled them to the creamery.

At Kolb's Hardware, my brother and I never tired of examining every detail of the shiny new bicycles in the window, dreaming of the day when we would own one.

Sometimes we made a special trip just to get barbershop haircuts. I liked the good-smelling tonic the barber rubbed in my hair.

Most of these trips were made in our Model T. But sometimes it was by horse and wagon, when we rode high on top a load of oats to be ground into meal at the elevator.

When winter came, our Model T was parked in the shed and the wagon box was transferred from its running gear to the chassis of the bobsled.

One time, two days before Christmas, Dad said he was going into Latimer and asked if we boys would like to go along. We eagerly said yes. We washed behind our ears, put on clean shirts and overalls, and bundled up against the cold. Dad slipped on large horsehide mittens to keep his hands warm while holding the reins. To pacify our little brother, who could not go along, we promised to bring home a surprise.

As we set out, Dad permitted us to tie our coaster behind the bobsled. It was great fun, with both of us sitting on the little sled, lurching along behind through the snowy ruts and drifts, trying to stay upright.

We enjoyed this sport for about the first two miles. By then, however, our fingers were tingling with the cold, and our toes felt like small, frozen potatoes inside our boots. So our sled and we were loaded onto the bobsled for the last mile into town.

Turning onto Main Street, with its few shops clustered near the Farmers Elevator, we were eager for the day's next adventure.

W e tied the team to the hitching rail beside Dohrman's store, then went inside. The double doors closed behind us, a bell tinkling its familiar greeting. The warmth and fragrance of the big store decorated for Christmas engulfed us.

My brother and I made straight for the floor grate over the furnace, where we dropped our wet mittens to dry and soaked up some of the welcome heat ourselves.

We then headed for the toy display. There was a little steam engine that really worked, as well as an electric train and a toy dragline. A paint box and sketchpad and a toy sewing machine also captured our admiration.

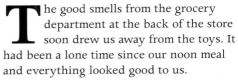

The good smells from the grocery department at the back of the store soon drew us away from the toys. It had been a lone time since our noon meal and everything looked good to us.

We lingered longingly over the cookies, the glass jars of candies—chocolates, jelly beans, orange slices, candy canes, and peanut brittle—along with the boxes of colorful hard candies that appeared only at Christmas. Boxes of fragrant apples and a crate of oranges added to the aroma.

Mr. Dohrman must have heard the growl of our empty stomachs for he selected two beautiful apples and gave one to each of us with a friendly wink and a "Merry Christmas!"

With our hunger somewhat appeased my brother and I got down to the serious business of selecting gifts we could afford for the family.

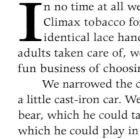

In no time at all we picked a small vase for Mom, a plug of Climax tobacco for Dad, a red bandana for Grandpa, and identical lace handkerchiefs for our grandmas. With the adults taken care of, we could then concentrate on the really fun business of choosing a toy for Little Brother.

We narrowed the choices down to a fuzzy stuffed bear and a little cast-iron car. We debated long and earnestly over the bear, which he could take to bed with him, and the car, with which he could play in the summertime on the roads we would make for him. Finally, we decided on the car *and* the bear. This used up all our coins, so we made a gentleman's agreement to postpone gifts for each other until next Christmas.

It was nearly dark when we left the store. Cheery lights glowed from windows of homes as we drove by. I thought of our own cozy home with its tree, decorated not with electric lights but with tinsel trimmings that reflected the light from our kerosene lamp.

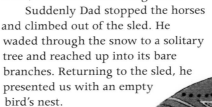

Suddenly my quiet reverie was shattered—we had forgotten the surprise for Little Brother! My brother and I wanted to turn right around and head back into town, but Dad would not go back.

Suddenly Dad stopped the horses and climbed out of the sled. He waded through the snow to a solitary tree and reached up into its bare branches. Returning to the sled, he presented us with an empty bird's nest.

Little Brother was delighted with his "surprise" and placed it in our Christmas tree, where he gazed at it until bedtime, dreaming of its former tenants.

TOYS
From Dad's Workshop

During most of the year, my brothers and I had access to Dad's workshop where we were free to experiment in our crude attempts at making things. A few weeks before Christmas, however, this fascinating place became closed to us.

After the chores were done and supper was over, Dad would put on his barn jacket and cap and disappear for the evening to his workshop. Sometimes Mom would join him while we kids, burning with curiosity and excitement, tried to occupy ourselves as best we could until Mom returned, aglow with some Christmas secret she and Dad shared.

From our upstairs bedroom we could see the yellow light of Dad's kerosene lantern shining from the workshop window. Thus, after Mom had tucked us in for the night, we were all set for pleasant dreams.

ARTLEY '88

No mansion or palace, with its many splendorous trappings of the season, could have offered more of the spirit and magic of Christmas than we, as children, experienced in the frugal surroundings of our farm home.

Those years, I was to learn later, were a period of financial hard times. There was barely enough money to pay for the necessities, let alone to indulge in extravagant giving that, even then, was becoming the vogue. We kids didn't know that, however. Isolated as we were on a little-used road of dirt (or mud, much of the year), our contacts were mostly with those in similar circumstances. We felt rich.

Even poring over the magazines and mail-order catalogs that came and seeing their illustrations of well-formed and lavishly decorated Christmas trees, with attractively wrapped gifts piled high beneath, only added to our enjoyment of the season. In no way did it detract from the appreciation we felt for our own spindly tree, with its meager, mostly homemade decorations, and the modest pile of gifts beneath.

Most often these gifts were of a practical nature, clothing or books. A few inexpensive toys or games would be found too, wrapped in brightly colored or white tissue paper and placed beneath the tree or among the fragrant pine boughs. I will not forget the happy Christmas we found a windup train on an oval track among the wrapped packages beneath the decorated tree.

But what made Christmases so extra special for us kids were the toys that came from Dad's workshop. Along with the wonderful fragrance of evergreen boughs, the scent of freshly worked pine and new paint (barely dry) is one that will forever bring to mind those magical Christmases of my youth.

The first toy I remember coming
from Dad's workshop was a
little red barn, complete with
fences and cutout wooden horses, cows,
and pigs. I must have been two years
old that Christmas. Dad played with
me on the floor showing me how to set
up the fences and put the cows in their
stanchions and the horses in their
stalls.

The next Christmas Dad made a
wooden pull-toy doe, jointed so that
it waggled when pulled. This toy was
mostly for Dean, who was a little over one
year old at the time. As I recall, Dad made
several of these toys, which were given to
some of our small cousins and friends.

A little table and two chairs came from Dad's shop the Christmas I was four and Dean was two. The bright red paint was barely dry Christmas morning and permeated the house with a new-paint smell. This small-size furniture was not only fun but practical as well and was used much by my brothers and me and by our small cousins and friends when they came to visit. Down through the years—after much use, repairs, and repainting—they have always remained "the little red table and chairs."

No farm is complete without a farmhouse. I must have been five the Christmas a toy house and a windmill came out of Dad's shop to join the little barn. Mom had made curtains to hang from the one window. Inside the little house was a store-bought cast-iron range. With it came an iron pot and skillet and an iron lifter that really worked for taking off the little stove lids. Also bought for the little house was a table and chair set stamped out of lithographed tin.

Under the little wooden windmill, with a wheel that turned in the wind, was a tiny iron pump. By working the little handle up and down, one could really pump water from and back into a small iron tank at its base.

In October, for his fifth birthday, Dean was given a toy locomotive made of heavy gauge metal. We both enjoyed playing with this toy, for it reflected our interest in the freight trains that daily passed through our neighborhood.

That year, as in others, there was the pain of anticipation and the fun of trying to guess what it was that Dad was making for us for Christmas. We heard the sounds of sawing, hammering, and sanding coming from the workshop. Both our parents teased us by giving us clues as to what the big secret was. They hinted that it was black and red and about six feet long. How we puzzled over that bit of information!

Then one day, shortly before Christmas, we were stopped at a railroad crossing waiting for a string of freight cars to pass. Mom called Dad's attention to a freshly painted boxcar passing before us. It was only after Christmas morning that Mom's seemingly innocent observation and Dad's acknowledgment of it had meaning for us.

The sight that greeted us that Christmas morning was one that would delight any child. Three wooden train cars, reeking of new paint and coupled to the familiar metal toy locomotive, almost dwarfed the Christmas tree and the meager supply of packages beneath. Dad had turned out a bright red boxcar, a black coal car, or gondola, and a caboose, also a bright red.

We spent many gleeful moments that day, not only examining and playing with the train, but also confronting our parents concerning the ambiguous clues with which they had teased us as the train was secretly being made in Dad's shop.

Most of the toys Dad made for us were just that, toys. They were not miniature scale models of the real thing. The last toy to come out of Dad's shop for Dean and me, however, was a little haystacker that really worked, in its own small way.

As we pulled the string over two small pulleys (which Dad had made by cutting down a couple of empty spools from Mom's sewing basket) the little stacker would lift a small bunch of cut grass and deposit it in a pile that was soon a little haystack. This activity, of course, had to wait until summer.

As the years passed and Dean and I grew older, Dad no longer made gifts for us. We had graduated to things like air rifles and skis. And, of course, books and clothes were still appreciated. But we did enjoy being in on the secrets: watching the progress of the toys Dad continued to make for our younger brother and cousins.

The Christmas after our little brother Dan turned six or seven, Dad made him a whole set of little farm buildings, including a house, barn, silo, hog house, corn crib, and machine shed. There were also some small village buildings: a church, depot, and general store. The round silo was carved from the limb of an ash tree. It had a domed roof and was painted to look like a clay block silo.

Dan and his playmates enjoyed these toys as much as Dean and I had ours. But he took better care of his and kept them for his children and now his grandchildren to enjoy.

I wish we still had the little farm buildings that Dad made for Dean and me. We would care for them as valued relics of our childhood. But, sad to say, the little house, barn, and windmill, much like their full-scale counterparts across the country, have disintegrated back into the earth from which they came. These toys, as well as others Dad made for us, have become a part of the soil beneath the shade of the maples where we so often played with them.

I suppose it is only in the maturity of our latter years that we value the artifacts of our lives as objects of historical value or treasured keepsakes. In hindsight, I cannot imagine why we didn't take better care of those heirlooms, which they certainly were. But as children we did value them highly as toys to use and to enjoy for that brief moment of childhood.